The Story of
Noah's Ark

by Caryn Rivadeneira

illustrated by Peter Grosshauser

SPARK
HOUSE
FAMILY

MINNEAPOLIS

A long, long time ago, an old, old man named Noah built a boat.

Every day, under a hot, hot sun, Noah sawed and sanded long planks of wood. He thwacked his hammer and nailed the planks into place. As he did, the shape of a giant boat rose out of the dry, dry land.

Noah did it because God had told him to. Noah loved and trusted God.

But not everyone
loved and trusted
God the way Noah did.
All the other people in the world had given
up goodness and turned toward badness—the
baddest kind of bad!

Instead of speaking kindly to one another, they said mean things.

Instead of helping one another, they hurt each other.

No one did what was right—ever!

No one obeyed God—ever!

Because no one loved God—not even the teensiest bit.

No one except Noah.

That's why God had told Noah something surprising, something startling, something shocking.

God said, "Noah, I am sad and mad. People have forgotten about me and turned away from what I want for my beautiful world. So I am unmaking what I made before. I'm going to bring lots and lots of rain to flood the whole earth. But you have remembered me, Noah. I want you to build a huge boat of cypress wood. Then gather your family and two of every kind of creature I have made. And I will keep you safe."

So Noah built the ark.

Noah's neighbors laughed and laughed. Noah's neighbors shook their heads. They pointed their fingers at Noah, stuck out their tongues, and called him names. Silly Old Noah, they thought, building a boat when there isn't a lake, a river, or a sea big enough to float it in for miles and miles around!

But Noah kept building. Every day, under the hot, hot sun, Noah sawed and sanded and thwacked even though his neighbors laughed and laughed, even though there was no water for miles and miles.

Then one day, the bright sky
darkened. The wind whistled
through the trees. Gray clouds
moved in from the west. Thunder
rumbled in the distance. Thick drops
fell from the sky. God had sent the rain.

Noah's neighbors stopped pointing and
laughing and sticking out their tongues. Instead,
they ran for their houses. They'd never heard such
thunder nor seen such rain, and they were terrified.

But not Noah. As the winds
whipped and the thunder
rumbled and the
rain plopped,

he pulled open the door to the ark and
called for his family.

Noah's wife stepped out of the house.

"Is it time?" Noah's wife asked.

"It is," Noah said.

Noah and his family carried baskets of clothes and food toward the ark.

The ground rumbled all around them. From all directions came animals—two of every sort, just as God had said. And two by two, camels and zebras, grizzly bears and llamas, elephants and mountain lions, pythons and koalas all slid and clomped and stomped into the boat.

Noah's eyes grew wide as the animals snuffed and snorted, cawed and hooted, growled and spat as they walked past Noah and his family.

Noah's stomach gurgled. His hands sweated. These were big animals with big roars and big teeth. Will they all fit in the ark? he wondered.

Noah watched the hyenas skulk and the baboons waddle toward the ark. Will they fight with each other? Will they bite me?

But Noah had built his ark exactly as God instructed. Noah trusted that God could fit them all, feed them all, and protect them all, just as God had said.

The rain kept falling and the animals kept coming. Drop by drop, two by two. Soon springs and rivers flowed through the land. The last animals—two slow sloths—crawled into the ark. Noah took one last look at the dry land below him and walked out of the ark.

And they all waited.

And waited.

For days and days as the rain poured and poured and the thunder cracked.

The winds whooshed and whistled outside the ark.

The water rushed and gurgled around them.

It rained for seven days. Then, suddenly, the
ark began to rock back and forth, back and forth.
Waves crashed against the bottom of the boat.

A wolf howled. A lion roared. A squirrel chattered. The animals were afraid. So were Noah and his family. They prayed that God would not forget them.

The boat stopped rocking as the water lifted it. They were floating! They were safe. Just as God had said.

The rain poured over the whole earth for forty days and forty nights. The water rose so high that it covered mountains. But the ark kept floating, and everyone and everything inside it kept warm and dry.

But it got loud in that boat! And stinky! All those animals, munching and slurping and growling, made Noah wonder when they were ever going to get out of the boat.

After months and months floating across the flooded earth, Noah noticed mountaintops far, far in the distance. The water must be going down! Noah was excited.

Then—screeeeeeech.

The ark had landed on . . . something!

Noah ran to look. He threw open a window
but saw only water. They were perched at the tip-
top of a mountain! There had to be more land
somewhere. So Noah let one of his ravens fly free.
But the raven came back to the ark. The ark was
still the driest place around. The raven perched on
the windowsill before flying off again.

Noah wouldn't give up. He trusted God. He
sent out his favorite milky-white dove, but it too
came right back. Every day, Noah could see a
little bit more of the mountain they rested on.
So seven days later, he sent the dove out again.
This time, it returned with an olive leaf
in its beak. The
dove had found
a tree!

Noah and his family danced and danced. They
sang and clapped to the animals, who just munched
and slurped and growled. God had saved them!

Noah sent his dove out one more time. The
dove never came back. But Noah wasn't sad.
This was good news! The dove had found
trees and dry ground and fresh worms. The
earth was drying out.

Day by day the water went down, down, down.

Then God said to Noah, "Come out of the ark! Bring your family and the animals!"

They were free. They were safe.

The animals stretched and sniffed as they climbed out of the boat. Some shoved and squirmed their

way toward the trees and rocks. None of them looked back as they headed down the mountain, two by two, back to the lands they came from.

Noah gathered rocks and stacked one on top of the other. Then he lit a fire on top of the stack as an offering of thanksgiving to God. God smelled the smoke from the fire and smiled. Noah knelt down on the ground and praised God.

Noah loved God. And God loved Noah.

God said to Noah, "Your children—and the pups and cubs and chicks from the animals on the boat—will once again fill this earth that I love. Even though I know people will forget me, I will remember them."

Noah looked up. An arc of red, orange, yellow, green, blue, indigo, and violet spread across the blue sky. Noah gasped. He heard a wolf howl and a lion growl in the distance. A squirrel chattered from the tree branch beside him. All creation noticed the beautiful rainbow.

Then God said, "I will never again flood the whole earth. When you see this rainbow in the clouds, I will see it too, and I will remember this promise between me and you and every living thing on the earth."

Making Faith Connections: A Note to Grown Ups

Sharing a Bible story with a child can be a wonderful way to grow your faith together. Here are a few suggestions to enrich a child's engagement and learning with this book.

The Story behind This Story

This picture book is based on the story of Noah from Genesis 6–9. Like much of the Old Testament, this part of the biblical narrative is not exactly kid-friendly. However, a caring adult can help kids enter the story in age-appropriate, imaginative ways.

God is so heartbroken by the fallen state of humanity that God destroys all of creation and starts over with Noah, his family, and a bunch of animals. In the end, God makes a covenant with Noah to never destroy the earth again. There are many parallels between this story and the creation stories in Genesis, particularly between Genesis 1:20-31 and Genesis 9:1-17. This can make for some interesting conversation with older children who are familiar with both stories.

Questions for Reflection

 What good choices did Noah make?

 God asked Noah to do a hard thing. Why did God want Noah to build an ark?

 What do you think it was like for Noah and his family to be on the ark with all those animals?

Would you like to be on board the ark? Why or why not?

 How did Noah show God that he was thankful? How do you show or tell God that you're thankful?

 Why did God send a rainbow? What do you think of when you see a rainbow?

Activities

Did you notice Squiggles, the expressive caterpillar who appears in this book? When you see Squiggles on a page, ask your child how Squiggles is feeling about what's happening in the story. Invite your child to talk about a time they felt the same way Squiggles does about something in their lives.

With paper and crayon (or marker), draw an animal you imagine was on the ark. Then talk about what Noah would have needed to have on board to take care of this animal.

Think of a "family promise." What's something you can promise one another? Design a symbol for the promise. It can be a rainbow or a star or a turkey or a unicorn or anything you want. Hang it somewhere in your home to remember the promise.

A Prayer to Say Together

God, thank you for your promise to love us and care for us even when we aren't at our best. Help us remember to be kind to others and to take care of the wonderful animals and this beautiful world. Amen.

First edition published 2016
Printed in United States
22 21 20 19 18 17 16   1 2 3 4 5 6 7 8

ISBN: 9781506417677

The Story of Noah's Ark
Written by Caryn Rivadeneira
Edited by Carla Barnhill
Cover design by Mighty Media
Cover illustration by Peter Grosshauser
Interior designed by Mighty Media
Illustrations by Peter Grosshauser

Library of Congress Cataloging-in-Publication Data

Names: Rivadeneira, Caryn Dahlstrand, author. | Grosshauser, Peter, illustrator.
Title: The Story of Noah's Ark : a Spark Bible Story / written by Caryn Rivadeneira; illustrated by Peter Grosshauser.
Description: First edition. | Minneapolis, MN : Published by Sparkhouse Family, 2016.
Identifiers: LCCN 2016006499 (print) | LCCN 2016010390 (ebook) | ISBN 9781506417677 (hardcover : alk. paper) | ISBN 9781506417783 (ebook)
Subjects: LCSH: Noah (Biblical figure)--Juvenile literature. | Noah's ark--Juvenile literature.
Classification: LCC BS580.N6 R57 2016 (print) | LCC BS580.N6 (ebook) | DDC 222/.1109505--dc23
LC record available at http://lccn.loc.gov/2016006499

VN0004589; 9781506417677; JUN2016

Sparkhouse Family
510 Marquette Avenue
Minneapolis, MN 55402
sparkhouse.org